ABOUT THE AUTHOR

Claire Timmermans, an Australian, is the world's most famous swimming instructor for babies and young children. The success of her methods has been reported in newspapers everywhere, including Russia. She is also featured in the film *Always a New Beginning,* which received an Oscar nomination.

How to Teach Your Baby to Swim

CLAIRE TIMMERMANS

STEIN AND DAY/*Publishers*/New York

First published in 1975
Copyright © 1975 by Claire Timmermans
Library of Congress Catalog Card No. 73-90707
All rights reserved
Designed by DAM
Printed in the United States of America
Stein and Day/*Publishers*/Scarborough House
ISBN 0-8128-1666-8
Paperback ISBN 0-8128-1946-2

I wish to dedicate this book to my very first pupils, our daughter Andrea and son Mark, who taught me more than I could ever teach them, and to my husband Tim, whose constant encouragement inspired me to continue.

ACKNOWLEDGMENTS

To Glen Doman, executive director of the Institutes for the Achievement of Human Potential in Philadelphia, at whose insistence I wrote this book.

To the late Ed Steet, our good friend for many years, who spent many weeks photographing all our babies, displaying his usual good humor and the patience of Job, as well as his photographic skill.

To Lee Pattinson, S.R.N., S.C.M., I.W.C., baby expert, and journalist, who helped me to rewrite this book.

To all those mothers who repeatedly traveled to our home so that we could film and photograph their babies.

To all those babies who came to my classes. To you, my little ones, a great big "thank you." You have taught me so much.

CONTENTS

INTRODUCTION

I am not writing this introduction under the pretense that I am an impartial witness to its contents. I am not. It is I who insisted that Claire Timmermans write this book.

There is now emerging a new sort of literature which is of vast importance directly to all parents and indirectly to many others as well. These books are written by people from many countries who have certain things in common:

—They are not professional writers.

—They are well known to each other.

—Each of them has a unique piece of knowledge about children.

—Each of them has an abiding respect for the ability of tiny children to learn—easily—things adults often learn only with great difficulty.

This small but important book is part of that literature.

Come visit the world with me. . . . Their Royal Highnesses, the Crown Prince and Princess of Japan, lead the waves of applause for a beautifully moving

11

rendition of Beethoven's Minuet in G. The most unusual thing about this national concert is that the three thousand musicians playing piano and stringed instruments range in age from three to ten years. They are students of that extraordinary Pied Piper, Shini-chi Suzuki. His book, *Nurtured by Love* (Exposition Press), is part of the new literature.

In the Philadelphia school system, which is no exception, some twenty to thirty percent of the children cannot read, or cannot read at grade level. Yet in the same city there are hundreds of severely brain-damaged two-year-olds who *can* read; who, in fact, would rather read than eat. They are among the many, many thousands of tiny children who are reading, the world over, thanks to the work of the Institutes for the Achievement of Human Potential. *How to Teach Your Baby To Read* (Random House), now published in a dozen languages, was the first book of the new literature.

In Rio de Janeiro tiny children do Instant Math, coming to conclusions before the adults around them have so much as framed the problem. Most adults who watch do not understand how the children can do Instant Math. The children do not understand how the adults can *not* do Instant Math.

These and other books that might be named all stress the ability of tiny children to learn anything easily, joyfully, and without conscious effort. They also stress the indispensability of the parent to this process.

How to Teach Your Baby to Swim is the latest addition to the new literature.

The swimming pool is in Melbourne, Australia; it's full, and it's a charming sight. There are a dozen beautiful bikini-clad young mothers and a dozen lovely babies. The mothers drop the babies into the water, the babies swim to the surface, and the mothers take them into their arms. The babies don't sputter or choke. They smile.

In this book, Claire Timmermans, a splendid mother, a superlative swimming teacher, and a vast respecter of children tells you step by step precisely how to teach your babies to swim. She does so with obvious warmth and dedication. She is pre-eminently qualified to do so, after years of successful experience.

Among other things, Claire emphasizes the importance of teaching babies to swim to help protect them from drowning—in itself an obviously splendid reason. But there are others, as readers of this book will discover for themselves.

I believe that all babies should be taught to swim. Why? Because learning to swim is one more step toward the confidence, the superiority that all children could enjoy if only we would give them the opportunity.

　　　　　—Glenn Doman, Director
　　　　　The Institutes for the Achievement of
　　　　　Human Potential

PREFACE

There is nothing new about teaching babies to swim. This was pointed out to me by Professor Raymond Dart, the anthropologist who discovered one of the missing links in the evolution of man.

"Claire," he told me, "what you are doing with babies is good, it's interesting, but it's not new. People on Pacific islands are doing it every day, and have been doing it for many generations. They think nothing of it. It's completely normal and natural to their way of living."

He is right, of course. And we can go back to the early Greeks and Romans and find references to taking babies into pools and teaching them to swim at a very early age.

So the kind of work I am doing with children is certainly not new. It just had to be rediscovered. But then, every great reform the world has known has come about not by doing something altogether new, but by making a new use of something old.

But why do I think it's important to teach babies to swim? Very few children under the age of two are capable of swimming to the side of a pool and getting out unaided; in other words, of saving themselves from drowning solely by their own efforts. But a child who has been accustomed to being in the water almost from birth has a very decided advantage over a child who has had no experience in water outside of a small bathtub—and a greater advantage still over one who has learned to fear water.

For one thing, he is less likely to panic if he should tumble unexpectedly into a pool or some other body of water. He is more likely to turn automatically on his back as he rises and to float unconcerned if he has been taught to do so. This in itself often means the difference between living and drowning: it gives an adult time to get to him.

At birth, every baby is a perfect swimmer. For nine months he has lived in the fluid world of the womb, which sounds like a comfortable one. The association between water and ease can be maintained and reinforced if the child is reintroduced to the element of water during his early days in the outer world.

The only difference between being in the womb and being in water after birth is the need for breathing. By placing a baby in a large amount of water at a suitable temperature, you allow him to re-experience the weightlessness of the days before he was born. Once again he can experience the comfortable, protective world he so recently left.

Newborn babies cannot be taught formal, stylized swimming movements. What early swimming lessons can teach them is how to relax and enjoy being in the water. In the process, they also develop balance, coordination, and strength (exactly as a crawling child does in the early stages of walking). By the time they are approximately two years old they will be able to swim—just as the unsteadily tottering toddler becomes the confidently running two-year-old.

One of my own greatest incentives to teach babies to swim is the happy faces that reward my work—not only the babies' faces but those of their mothers as well. As one mother said, "I know Judy enjoys it and I find myself looking forward to having her all to myself to cuddle and play with for half an hour in the water."

A Note on Competition

Teaching a child to swim should not necessarily be regarded as a first step toward competitive swimming.

I know very few children who have an inborn sense of competition. There are some who will turn almost any game into a test of superiority, but most children are happier when they play for the fun of it.

Considerable harm is done by parents who compare one child with another. Such comparisons often destroy a genuine friendship because they plant seeds of discontent in the mind of the child unable to match the achievement of his friend.

No one expects any two people of thirty to be exactly alike in their abilities, yet many people see nothing incongruous in expecting a two-year-old to have the same abilities as any other two-year-old. No two children develop in exactly the same way at exactly the same rate. Each should be permitted to develop at his own pace, in accordance with his own capabilities.

It is important to understand that progress follows encouragement. I have seen children really enthusiastic about swimming and progressing well, only to be set back by their mothers' comparisons: "See how well Jimmy floats. Why can't *you* do it like that?"

My husband and I once received photos and press clippings from a teacher of swimming for babies in Germany. The headlines read, "Little Girl of Two Breaks World Record"; "Baby of 5 Months Sets World Flotation Record." Accompanying correspondence asked for information on records set by Andrea, our daughter. Without hesitation I replied, "None." I do not feel that records are of any importance as such. Our *children* are important, not the feats they perform.

Part One

How My Career Started

As far as my work of teaching babies to swim is concerned, I have been fortunate in the men in my life: my husband and my father.

My Dutch father was a famous water polo player in the 1930s, when he represented Holland in international competitions. Because of his size (he was always double the average weight for his years) he was known as Fat Peter, but he could just as easily have been called the Gentle Giant, for though he was outstandingly strong, he was also extremely gentle. My four sisters and I always loved to be in the pool with him. We adored playing with him, crawling over the big tummy rising like a rounded iceberg from the water.

Today when dealing with children in my classes I follow the principles he laid down in those days. His ideas are perhaps best illustrated by an incident that occurred when I was about four years old. I was sitting by the side of the pool when one of his friends picked me up and started to toss me into the water. I screamed and Dad asked what was going on.

"No daughter of Fat Peter is going to sit near a swimming pool without going into it," his friend said with a laugh.

This brought from my father the most commanding tone I'd ever heard him use.

"My daughter will get into the pool when she's good and ready. Now put her down and leave her alone!"

I realized later how wise he was. Had he allowed me to be thrown in, I might never have come back to the water happily. As it was, I was swimming within a year of the incident.

I was almost fourteen when my parents migrated to Australia, and at seventeen I was granted an Education Department studentship that brought me to Melbourne to train as a teacher. Because of the proximity of Melbourne University, where I was studying, to the City Baths, an indoor swimming pool, I started to swim there. One of the coaches, Ann Timmermans, agreed to coach me, and later introduced me to her brother Tim, whom I was to marry.

When I was almost twenty-one and close to graduation, Ann was killed in an automobile accident. Her death drastically changed my life. Instead of going on to teach in a high school (for which I was qualified), I decided to carry on with Ann's work. I had seen how much enjoyment her swimming lessons had brought to so many children, and she had taught me her methods. Encouraged by Tim, I set about continuing with them.

Tim and I were married soon afterward and started our own swim school. After six years it was established firmly enough so that I could stop teaching for a time to start a family. A year later Andrea was born.

The Family Bathtub

Unfortunately, complications following the birth left me very weak—so weak that I had difficulty in caring for Andrea, especially in such tasks as bathing her. We had the usual small baby bath, the kind of portable tub that is filled with water and placed on a table. I found bathtime tiring and extremely awkward. The table was too high to permit me to handle Andrea with ease, so we tried putting the bath on a chair. This was too low and equally awkward. By the time Andrea was bathed and fed, I was ready for bed myself.

Tim remembered a couple he had known who always bathed their baby in the family bathtub, so we decided to try this. We filled the tub to about three inches from the top. I knew that because of the depth of the water Andrea would float. I also knew that newborn babies needed support under their necks, as the muscles were not yet strong enough to support their heads unaided, so I kept one hand under Andrea's neck as I lowered her into the tub.

I was delighted to see she loved it. I gently moved her backward and forward, and her expression showed me her complete acceptance of this new style of bathing. She had a look of serene relaxation.

And this system was much more comfortable for

me. I knelt on the floor beside the tub, my left arm along its edge while I supported Andrea's neck with my right hand, my arm only slightly extended. I let her ears go under the water but kept her face above the surface so that she was in a perfect floating position, her weight carried completely by the water. The procedure was much less tiring for me, as I didn't have to support her weight.

Her obvious happiness, combined with my comfortable, relaxed position, made time fly by. I suddenly realized that twenty minutes had passed. Quickly I rubbed her all over with soap, rinsed her, and lifted her out. Soon she was in bed fast asleep. For my part, I was exhilarated instead of exhausted. After I had put her to bed I sailed through the washing of the day's accumulation of diapers, and from that day I never bathed her in anything but the family tub.

Ten days after Andrea and I had arrived home from the hospital a heat wave struck the city. In Melbourne, that means temperatures ranging from 95 to 115 degrees Fahrenheit. I remembered vividly that during a three-day heat wave the previous year, nineteen babies had died from dehydration.

We were determined to keep our baby not only alive but happy during the hot weather. I had read as much as I could about ways of preventing dehydration, and the suggestions of one registered nurse made great sense to me. She told mothers to fill the bathtub with lukewarm water and let their babies soak in it, keeping them cool and avoiding dehydration at the same time. She advised leaving the water in the tub during the day and dipping the baby into it anytime he appeared to be affected by the heat, adding a little warm water from time to time to keep the temperature at a steady 90 degrees Fahrenheit.

I followed her instruction, filling the tub to the brim by six o'clock in the morning. As soon as Andrea woke I gave her the first bath of the day, then fed her and put her back in bed naked, with two diapers spread out under her. I noticed that she began to perspire as she slept, and as soon as she awoke I put her back into the water for half an hour. The first day of the heat wave she spent a total of at least four hours in the bathtub.

The second day brought even higher temperatures. I was extremely uncomfortable while I was bathing Andrea, so I got in the tub with her. Sheer bliss!

I did it again later in the afternoon. It was getting close to her feeding time, and she started to push her face against me. She soon found what she was seeking, and started sucking. She emptied one breast completely, then was burped and started on the other side.

It made sense, I realized later. During the hot days we both became hot and sticky at feeding times as our skin touched. In the bath we were both kept cool by the water. I breast-fed her for five months and found she was always most content after she had been fed in the bath. Was it possible that the coolness of her body made digestion of the milk easier?

The heat wave lasted five days and Melbourne's babies sweltered and suffered. Because Andrea and I spent most of those days in the tub, we both came through it well and happy.

After the worst of the heat wave was over we continued with our regular baths, and as Andrea moved her arms and legs in the water I decided to experiment a little. I created waves by moving her backward and forward, gently lifting her above a wave coming from her feet but letting one from the top of her head wash over her face, then holding her upright immediately. I expected objections but she didn't even look surprised.

The Swimming Pool

She was about six weeks old when I went around to our swimming pool to cool off. I placed Andrea beside the pool in her baby bouncer, but her gestures and noises obviously indicated that she wanted to join me. As our pool is used for teaching purposes, it is indoors and heated, with the temperature kept at approximately 90 degrees; so I took her into the water.

She enjoyed it as much as she enjoyed the tub at home, so from then on I took her with me whenever I went, which was almost daily.

I never took her into the pool while classes were being held, but apparently someone saw her with me just the same. I received a phone call from one of Melbourne's leading newspapers. The journalist who called asked if it was true that I was teaching my baby to swim. I said it was, and asked him how he had heard about it. He declined to say and I never did find out who told him, though I can guess why: the newspapers give a lottery ticket to anyone who phones in a tip on a story that is used.

The paper wanted permission to take pictures, and when we agreed to this we were visited by a reporter and a photographer. The result was a large front-page picture of Andrea and a double spread of photos and articles in the center pages.

Australian magazines were quick to pick up the story, and articles were syndicated around the world. We received press clippings from Japan, South China, Germany, Holland, England, and the United States. Television and newsreel crews came to film Andrea. She took the situation calmly, acting like an experienced trouper in front of the cameras, swimming for them, smiling, and showing off all her little water tricks.

I expected the publicity to die down once the first wave was over, but instead it intensified and we received mail from people all over the world who wanted to know how they could teach their own babies to swim. Special interest was roused in Germany, Holland, and England, where Andrea appeared in a newsreel that was shown in movie theaters.

Local people, too, began to get in touch with me, and the phone rang constantly, nearly always with the same question: "Will you please teach my baby to swim?"

Tim and I had to take stock of the situation.

Officially, I was out of the swimming business. I

had retired so that I could fully enjoy raising a family. Tim left the decision up to me. If I wanted to work with babies, that was fine with him. If I didn't, that was fine, too.

I was learning so much each day from my work with Andrea that the idea of teaching other small babies fascinated me, and I decided to take on a few pupils as an experiment.

Once I had decided to accept them and had committed myself to teaching them, I knew I was also committed to making as good a job of it as I possibly could. I planned to do as much research as I could, only to discover there were no books or written records of any kind on teaching babies to swim.

As a result, my only research was Andrea.

I would say to her, "Darling, I don't know just what to do or how to do it. So will you please help? When I do something you don't like, let me know. When you do like it, let me know that, too."

I learned that if I watched her expressions and reactions very closely she was doing just that. One of the things she clearly liked was being dunked underwater. I tried several ways of doing this and found that if I told her by actions as well as by words that it was about to happen, she prepared herself.

My method of "warning" her was to lift her up a little, then blow on her face. She would close her eyes against the rush of air and I would duck her under while her eyes and mouth were still closed. Sometimes she took in just a drop or two of water, and she would immediately push this out of her mouth as she rose.

My First Classes

When I first started classes for babies I decided to take them individually, so that I could give each one my undivided attention.

I found that some babies took so long to get used to me that I couldn't even get them into the water happily until they had been to the pool two or three times, and even then as soon as I tried to handle them in the same way as I had done with Andrea they would start to cry.

I was gentle, I was loving—but it wasn't enough.

Some babies came for a few weeks, then when they started teething they cried the moment they left their mothers' arms.

I was fast becoming disillusioned and discouraged. Why couldn't these babies do what mine had done? Surely Andrea wasn't totally different from all the other babies I took into the pool with me.

Then I began to wonder if I had been right in thinking babies could be taught to swim. For eight years I had taught people from children of four years to adults of eighty, and had been outstandingly successful with all age groups. What was so different about babies?

I had heard there were people in Los Angeles who had been teaching babies to swim, and that lessons had been given there for the past twenty-five years, so I decided to travel to California.

I visited two schools for young children. At the first one, I saw a large number of instructors each teaching a baby. Some of the children were obviously happy and swimming outstandingly well, but I noticed one thing: all of the happy children were from two and a half to five years old. Most of the real babies—those between about six months and two years—were crying.

One mother was sitting by the side of the pool with a ten-month-old baby in her arms. Though she was holding him, he continued to cry. I noticed his eyes were focused on one particular instructor who wore sunglasses and a large hat to shade her face from the glare of the sun. As the mother began to hand the child over to this instructor, his crying became almost hysterical. I expected the teacher to speak to him soothingly, but to my surprise she dunked him under the water. He came up spluttering and coughing, and just as he took a breath and resumed crying the teacher dunked him again. I was amazed to see that neither mother nor teacher seemed to be at all disturbed by his cries.

Certainly I'd been in the habit of giving Andrea consecutive dunkings also—but only when she was happy. I would *never* dunk her otherwise. But that baby kept on crying and being dunked right through his whole lesson.

After the crying baby had left the pool, I suggested to Andrea that she might like to swim over to the teacher, who was then free. Andrea refused, clinging to me like a limpet, and suddenly it struck me that the adults knew that the instructor was merely a lady wearing sunglasses and a hat, but to our babies she must have looked little short of a monster. Only her head was visible above water; she was very tanned, and the glasses and huge hat obscured her face and distorted her appearance. No wonder Andrea wouldn't go near her!

I visited the second swim school the following Sunday morning. We arrived to find about twenty-five or thirty babies and young children there. Andrea and I went into the pool with friends who had come with us, and Andrea happily swam from me to them and back again.

The head of the school pointed out one child, only three and a half years old, who was doing a beautiful crawl stroke, then a four-year-old who dived off the one-meter board and swam the length of the pool in a perfect butterfly stroke with a dolphin kick. His little body moved with as good coordination as I had seen in world champions.

This restored my faith in what little children could do—until I looked at the other end of the pool, where the little babies were. Again, most of them were crying.

Andrea, at seven and a half months, was the youngest baby present on that Sunday morning, but for two and a half hours she frolicked in the water while older babies howled. She was under the surface oftener than above it, and she loved every minute. The only time she cried was when she had to come out and get dressed.

The Breakthrough

I returned to Australia and started receiving phone calls from mothers wanting to resume their babies' lessons. But I was not at all sure I wanted to resume them. Babies in the pools of swimming schools all seemed to be unhappy; the only successful teaching I had seen had been done in people's own swimming pools. Unfortunately, few people in Melbourne have heated outdoor pools. I couldn't force myself to work with unhappy babies.

So the decision was made: I would *not* teach any babies except my own.

The next few weeks were bliss. I went into the pool only with Andrea and we enjoyed every minute we spent there together. We laughed and played and let the rest of the world go by. How marvelous it was to be a mother!

Often Tim came into the water to join us, and those were the best times. I felt privileged to have such good communication with my healthy, suntanned, beautiful ten-month-old daughter. Life was just for us to live together; the three of us felt little need for any social life.

I was brought rather abruptly out of this pleasant lotus land by a mother who phoned with the usual request, that I teach her baby. My refusal was greeted with an approach new to me. Very upset, she said, "I think you're terribly selfish!" Taken aback, I asked her what she meant, and she said, "When your little girl is four years old, she'll be able to swim. We have a large property with three ponds on it. When our little boy is four, he could drown in one of them."

She then made a request that seemed to be an adequate compromise and assuaged any guilt I might have felt: "Please, won't you let me come to your pool just to watch what you do with your baby? Then I'll be able to copy it with mine."

This seemed a practical solution. I didn't in the least mind having someone copy me. I just didn't want to do the actual teaching.

The next day she joined us with her baby and I gave her a few basic instructions. She worked on these and copied what I was doing. Within three weeks her baby had progressed as far as Andrea had done in the same time. After that it was all plain sailing.

Another mother joined us with her baby, on the same understanding. We met at the pool twice a week, like a little team with me as captain. I explained the basic fundamentals of swimming; then we pooled our ideas about their application to babies.

And all of a sudden I had the answer to the problem that had been bothering me.

I didn't have to teach babies to swim at all.

Their own mothers were doing it and being far more successful than I had been. All I had to do was to train the mothers and supervise!

The Classes Grow

That one phone call from a worried mother was the start of what eventually became a full-time project.

Our initial small team continued to work at home. Each mother would try out the exercises we did, either at home or at the beach, then report back to me. Her experience was used to help others, and many variations of the same fundamental exercise were done to make the lessons more interesting for the children. This system enabled us to find out what an individual baby liked. We discovered, for example, that there are at least twelve ways to hold a baby lying on his back.

As news of our work spread, I received requests from other mothers anxious to join us and learn how to be the teachers of their own babies. Within a few months we had about seventy babies coming twice a week.

Then we struck a problem. Many of the mothers had to travel long distances (at least fifteen mothers had to drive an hour each way to and from our pool). Classes became too time-consuming for many of them; for a single half-hour lesson they needed to be absent from home for approximately three hours, so they had to set aside a total of at least six hours a week, sometimes more.

We tried changing the schedule, having only one lesson a week, but found that we frequently had to give the children at least ten minutes to warm up before they could start their exercises, instead of being able to carry on immediately where we had left off the previous lesson.

There were some, however, who didn't appear to need any warm-up, and we found that those who were making steady progress were those who were bathed in a *full* bathtub at home. Their mothers encouraged them to blow bubbles and to lie on their tummies or backs as they did in the pool during swimming lessons. Because of the repetition of these activities at home, the continuity of the lessons was not interrupted.

Mark's First Swim

When Andrea was about fifteen months old I was pregnant again, and booked into one of the large maternity hospitals in Melbourne. This meant I would have an opportunity to collect firsthand data right from the very start, with a newborn baby.

I discussed with my obstetrician my plans to have the baby swim as soon as possible after birth; he agreed, and spoke to the nurse in charge of the maternity wing. She was agreeable after I told her that all I wanted was the use of an ordinary bathtub; if a newborn baby is allowed to float in a full tub the effect is the same as a swimming pool to an adult.

I arranged for a film to be made of the first swim to be taken by our yet-to-arrive baby, and while we waited I kept on teaching mothers with their babies. The heavier I became as pregnancy advanced, the more I enjoyed the time I spent in the water. The feeling of weightlessness was bliss, and the moment I entered the water all the abdominal pressure was relieved. I discovered firsthand why so many of the pregnant mothers attending classes had given audible sighs of relief as they lowered themselves into the water.

I taught classes for five hours the day before I went into the hospital. Then, on October 26, 1967, our second baby was born—a son, Mark Anthony. Although he was sixteen days premature, he weighed seven pounds and four ounces. His birth was normal and the pediatrician who examined him pronounced him complete and healthy.

He was born at 10 P.M., so I thought it sensible to postpone his initial swim till the following morning, when it would fit in with general hospital routine.

I was due for a disappointment. At the last moment the nurse refused to cooperate, even though Mark and I had both been examined by the doctor and pronounced fit enough to go ahead, and even though we had signed a release that relieved the hospital of any responsibility. That was all very well, it seemed, but if something went wrong, the hospital would receive adverse publicity.

My obstetrician backed me up to the point of transferring Mark and me to another hospital, where the head nurse proved more than helpful. She ordered the nursing staff to cooperate fully, and one room was cleared of all beds and a circular portable wading pool was set up with lights and cameras in position around it.

By the time the new arrangements could be made, Mark was three days old. When I undressed him for his first swim he started to cry (probably because of the temperature change, as the air was rather cool). The pool, five feet in diameter and ten inches deep, was filled with warm water. The moment I lowered Mark into its comfortable depths he stretched out. I supported his neck with my hand and he took up a perfect floating position: ears in the water; face, tummy, and toes out; body and legs near the surface.

In this position Mark fell fast asleep as I gently moved him backward and forward. The film crew was astonished, as were the nurses who came along to watch. He was not in the least disturbed by the strong lights, the noise of the cameras, or the voices of the people around him.

Andrea, then twenty-two months old, insisted on getting into the pool beside Mark, and played happily for the next twenty minutes while I was interviewed. I then created some waves and let one flow over Mark's face, but he stayed fast asleep. He woke at the second wave but just looked around and moved his arms and legs in the water with no sign of distress or discomfort. He had been in the water for thirty-five minutes when I finally lifted him out.

The next day we repeated the performance, and again it was filmed. His reaction was exactly the same as it had been on the previous day.

We went home when Mark was seven days old. One of the nurses gave me a copy of the records that had been kept since Mark's arrival at the hospital, and one fact revealed by those records was most interesting: on the two days that Mark had his "swim" he had taken the most nourishment, slept the longest, and put on the most weight.

When we left the hospital we went straight to our teaching pool, where we stayed in the water for twenty minutes. Then we went home and Mark settled down for a long sleep.

Mark has loved the water ever since. At least once a day I would give him a bath in a full tub, and I often got into the bath with him. He loved to be fed in the water, as Andrea had done, and once or twice a week I took him into the swimming pool.

His "historic" swim was featured in media all over the world, and once again we received requests

for advice and instructions from parents and professional people everywhere.

Experience has shown me that there are many
possible reasons for parents' wishing their children to
be taught to swim at an early age.

The child's safety is one motive. This is particularly important in Australia, where easy access to
beaches or rivers and the fast growth of family
swimming pools expose babies and many young
children to what could be fatal accidents.

Or they may simply love the water and would
delight in seeing their children enjoy it, too.

But there is one motive that is definitely a wrong
one. Some of the mothers in my classes in Australia
seemed to want to have their children learn how to
swim for the sake of some kind of status. They
wanted to be able to say that their children could
swim before they could walk, as though this were an
accomplishment of their own.

This attitude often leads to a very destructive
approach to teaching your baby how to swim. For
example, one mother I know wanted fast results at all
costs. Not only was she rough in her handling of her
child, but she was inconsiderate of the little girl's
feelings, always talking down to her, criticizing her
failures, and never giving her credit for any progress
she did achieve. Naturally enough, her little girl was
frightened and completely lacking in confidence.
When I held her she clung to me for dear life. I
handled her with care and after a few lessons could

feel her beginning to relax. I am convinced I could have had that child happy in the water and confident about swimming if I had been permitted to do it gradually, in my own way. But I would not push the child beyond her capabilities, and I told her mother so. The mother promptly canceled the lessons, saying she would take her little girl to a swimming teacher who would teach her to swim "without all this pussyfooting."

It's what that mother called "pussyfooting" that I have found to be of the utmost importance in successfully teaching a baby to swim, and your baby is no exception. Progress is achieved by taking very small steps and taking them slowly. With a happy, confident child you have a head start on two-way communication. If you attempt to introduce a step that is a little too advanced, a confident child will not hesitate to say, "I can't do that *yet!*" or "Can you show me again?" But a child who is lacking in confidence or is frightened can't express his doubts so openly; he will either refuse to try or try and fail and thus lose a little more of his already scanty confidence.

Before a frightened child is asked to perform any physical task, he has to be prepared for it mentally. The best way to do this is to be honest with the child. He should *never* be tricked into trying anything new.

If your child is frightened, my advice is, "Imagine yourself in your child's place."

Remember, you not only have to teach your child's body to swim. You have to prepare his *mind* as well.

Where Does Fear of Water Come From?

Many modern homes, especially apartments, are equipped with either shower stalls or small tubs. A baby often never even gets a chance to find out what it's like to float effortlessly in a (comparatively) large expanse of water.

Where a full-sized tub is available, accidents may occur which the child holds the water responsible for. Soapy water may hurt his eyes and some may enter his mouth and taste unpleasant. He is too young to differentiate between clear and soapy water; all he has learned from the experience is that if you put your head underwater, your eyes sting and you choke and it tastes awful.

The children of nonswimming parents are even more likely to learn to fear water. It is natural for parents to protect their young, and the most constructive way is to show them incipient dangers and guide them in ways of coping with them. But if parents can't cope with a potential problem themselves, they can't teach a child to do it, so the only solution is to avoid it. This is what most nonswimming parents do. They know they would be incapable of saving their children if they were in danger of drowning, so they say, "Don't go near the water or you'll drown." A child has to hear this only a few times before he believes it.

On the other hand, some toddlers, unable to swim, have indeed been drowned after they have jumped into water without any hesitation. Their action puzzled me for some time until a logical explanation for it occurred to me. Most mothers bathe their babies in a conventional baby bath; then when the transfer is made to a full-sized tub, they put only a few inches of water in it. Thus, the only water the child is exposed to is the amount he feels while he sits or lies on the base of the tub—just enough to splash about in and have fun. He never experiences the weightlessness of a large body of water and his mental picture of water is one of security and happiness: security because he has always been supported by the base of the bath and happiness because all he has ever known of water was its use as a plaything.

This, of course, is a false image, but the child is not aware of this. He is quite likely to jump into a large mass of water with no idea of the danger there. And if it is deep, he will be taken completely by surprise. For the first time in his life he will be going underwater. Feeling water go up your nose and into your mouth when you are expecting it is bad enough. To have this happen when you are taken unawares is a frightening experience. In addition to this, he is suspended in a mass of water and experiencing complete weightlessness for the first time in his life. He has no idea how to cope with that. There is no tub bottom to sit on. What's happened?

How can a parent avoid creating an atmosphere of fear and distrust, or banish it if it is already present? Even if the child is already past the toddler stage, it's not too late.

The first step is to make every bathtime a happy, constructive playtime. There should be no attempt to

regard the bathtime as a lesson period. You don't tell
a child what to do, you show him. When you get into
the tub with your youngster, let him see you enjoying
the water. If you are apprehensive about water, your
child will help you get over your fear while mastering
his own. Your attitude should be, "Come on, Johnny,
let's do this together. If other people can learn to love
and master the water, so can we!"

Part Two

When Should Your Baby Start Learning to Swim?

It is often necessary to restrict a young baby to the bathtub at home for his initial lessons. Here you can control the temperature of the water. There are few swimming pools warm enough for a newborn infant, who needs water at a temperature of about 90 degrees—too warm for older children or adults. Babies lose body heat at a much faster rate than older children and adults, as their heat-control centers are not fully mature, and water cools the body much faster than air does. As a baby gets older he gains weight and is less affected by cold. Then he is ready for the transfer to the pool.

Try to take your baby to a pool regularly while he is still too young to enter it. Just sit by the pool to accustom him to the noise. I have known a number of babies of four or five months who had been handled correctly by their mothers at home and who loved the water but were terrified by the noise when they first came to a pool.

When a baby stretches his arms out in the bath and barely has room to do it because he is touching both sides of the tub, he is ready for a larger body of water. He can still have his daily bath and playtime in the tub, but he can profit now by being taken to a pool at least once a week.

It's a lucky baby whose parents know how to play with him. When parents enjoy the company of their children fully, both children and parents reap many benefits. Children can learn anything through playing, and their achievements can give the parents tremendous satisfaction, particularly when it is obvious that the children are learning happily.

This parent-child relationship is extremely important in the teaching of swimming. When the relationship is sound, both teaching and learning become fun.

I don't think any child can learn positively or retain much of what is told to him while he is unhappy. He will neither understand what is being taught nor remember it for future use. Who wants to remember an unhappy experience?

Children who are happy and confident in the water will always be able to think themselves out of difficult situations in it, and are thus not likely to give way to panic, with its possibly tragic conclusion. This is why I feel that the way they actually move their arms and legs in the water is of little importance. The really important thing is the way their minds react.

A child learning to swim must be comfortable and relaxed. You should check the water in a pool yourself before taking him in. The ideal temperature is 90 degrees Fahrenheit. Chlorine is another thing you should check on. Submerge yourself completely, then open your eyes underwater. If the water stings your eyes, it will sting your baby's eyes, too.

If the temperature of the water is comfortable and there is no chemical condition to affect him adversely, yet he still reacts with some show of fear, the cause could be noise or activity around the pool to which he is not accustomed. In this case, simply cuddle him tightly to reassure him and reinforce his confidence.

The lessons I teach are usually best begun when a baby is about two or three weeks old, though they are still quite effective for any age up to about four years. The older the baby, however, the more careful you need to be about his handling. He should not have a new procedure forced on him when he would rather be doing something else. An older baby forms definite play habits, and while the first lesson as outlined in this book will be acceptable to a young baby, one of seven months or so will not be quite so docile. He will probably want to turn over on his tummy or move his arms and legs.

It is wise to work with a baby in approximately three to four feet of water. You will find you have maximum control over your movements if you crouch down until your shoulders are underwater. Do not kneel down; this makes you more likely to lose your balance. Keep on your feet with your knees bent.

Common sense should dictate the application of the lessons. You may proceed from one to the next whenever you feel your baby is ready for it. If he is showing interest in the breathing exercises but is reluctant to float on his back, proceed with the breathing and tummy exercises.

Remember, a good teacher is flexible. She does not make a baby conform to a set pattern, but uses the knowledge she has gained in the manner that best suits the baby she is teaching. Your baby's reaction is your most valuable guide. Work *with* your baby. Suggestion works better than force.

The lessons in this book are designed to make your baby safe in the water. They make no attempt to teach a baby formal swimming strokes. But this course of lessons *will* enable him to stay alive in many of the potentially dangerous situations involving water.

Progress should be slow, steady, and sure. If you see that some new step you introduce is making your baby uneasy, do not force him on, but go back over some particular work you have already covered which he enjoys.

Never attempt to introduce too much new material in any one lesson. A new movement should not be practiced more than twice at the initial lesson. It can be perfected in later sessions.

If you do not rush your baby, but concentrate on keeping him comfortable and happy at all times, you will find his progress quite satisfactory. Forcing him to attempt to do something for which he is not yet ready could undo what you have already established.

Although an older baby will at first make more demands on your patience, you will be compensated by the more rapid progress he makes, particularly in the first few lessons. Do not hold him back or you will find he will become bored and lose interest.

The opposite is true of a baby who begins lessons at a very early age. If he is forced on too quickly, his confidence in the water will be destroyed. He should spend at least two weeks consolidating each new step before moving to the next one.

Remember, however, that you, his mother or father, are the best judge of his capabilities. As long as you allow yourself to be guided by his reactions, you will retain his confidence and will be constantly adding to the natural advantages you already have.

Always, when teaching your baby, accentuate the positive and ignore the negative. When your baby tries to do what you are showing him, compliment him on his effort, not on the final result.

If you encourage him, you will eventually achieve the result you want. If you discourage him, he will lose heart and stop trying. You will have achieved nothing, and it will be difficult to persuade him to try again.

Caution without Panic

Most children are naturally adventurous, and any child learning to swim will at some time wander into water that is too deep for him.

He must be returned to the shallow water without being given a fright in the process. So, until your child is a capable swimmer, you *must* be in the water with him. You have to explain to your child which part of the water is deep and which part is shallow, but you must not make the deep water a frightening thing. Just explain to him that deep water is something he can't cope with *yet,* and continue to be watchful so that you can steer him away from trouble.

Because swimming is very much a family activity, you will find that children usually react in the water as they do at home. If a child enjoys his father's company more than his mother's, he will benefit from spending as much time as possible in the pool with his father, going with his mother only when his father is not available. If he appears to be really unhappy in the water with his mother, it is better to leave the lessons to the father completely.

Some fathers are rather boisterous with children, and this often tends to frighten them. In this situation it is often better for the mother to do the groundwork and build up the child's confidence; then when he is a capable swimmer he is more likely to appreciate the roughhouse play of his father.

In short, the child will tell you what is best for him.

The Nonswimming Parent

I have said that the best teachers for most children are their own mothers, though there are a few exceptions.

Particular care has to be taken when the mother herself fears the water. There is a great risk of her passing her fear to the baby unless she tackles the problem constructively.

If a mother cannot swim herself, she is not likely to have the confidence she needs to teach her baby to swim without some additional advice.

If you are one of those mothers, you would do well to tackle the problem as early as possible so that you will overcome your own fears while your child is still a confident baby. An older baby or small child is very quick to recognize fear or lack of confidence in an adult.

Go into about three feet of water (the shallow end of most pools is at this level) and crouch down till your shoulders and those of your baby are just submerged. Hold him very tightly against your body; he will feel secure, and for some reason this act has a similar effect on mothers.

Be content at first just to crouch in the water for a time. There is no need to rush things. When you get the feel of being in the water you can start to move around, still crouched down in shallow water and still holding your baby.

Then you can start blowing a few bubbles with your mouth just under the water. If you prefer, you can move to shallower water and sit down to do this. With a little practice you will find you can blow bubbles with both your mouth and your nose underwater. In time you will let your face go a little deeper.

Remember that this is a very gradual process, and you must always stay in shallow water so that you can have complete control over your movements. There is no need for a nonswimming mother to step boldly into deep water and start lessons. She, like her baby, has to progress slowly and feel confident. For this reason her initial lessons involve nothing more than submerging her shoulders in the water, staying at the shallow end, and holding her baby tightly against her.

I have tremendous respect for nonswimming mothers who subdue their own fears in order to teach their babies. I remember one in particular. She was about ten years older than the average mother in our classes, and Jason was her first child.

Because of an experience in her own childhood, she was so afraid of water that she found it impossible to relax. Jason was already nine months old when he came to his first class, so I could not take him from her.

She started to follow the normal course of instructions, but was so tense that she stiffened every time she put her mouth to the water to blow bubbles. Her fear was reflected in Jason's behavior, and he was very unhappy in the water.

I suggested that she forget about formal lessons for the time being, and for several months she just came and spent the time playing with Jason in the shallow end of the pool. Now and then she was able to bring herself to blow a few bubbles, and as she became friendly with other mothers in the class she began to relax a little more.

Because the atmosphere was happier, Jason started to enjoy himself more. He watched other children and eventually decided to try for himself a few of the things they were doing. Our worries were past history then.

It took Jason longer to learn to swim than most children—but if a stranger had tried to teach him, he might well have been frightened forever.

Interruptions in the Lessons

Val was one of the first to get in touch with me after the publicity about Andrea. She had a small son, Bruce, a few weeks older than Andrea, and about five months old by the time he took his first swimming lesson. At that time Val lived an hour and a half by car from our pool, so that for a half-hour lesson she had to be away from home more than four hours altogether. Nevertheless Bruce progressed wonderfully in the early lessons.

Then he had to go into a hospital for a few days to correct a slight malformation of one hand. He missed only three lessons, so we expected him to settle back quite happily. We were startled to find that Val could do nothing with him; he just cried and whimpered and clung to her.

Since then we have had several babies who have had to be hospitalized for varying periods of time and *all* of them suffered a tremendous blow to their confidence. We found that those babies whose mothers were prepared to give them undivided attention and love recovered from their hospital experiences most quickly. The mothers who became irritated by their babies' continual crying and whimpering needed much more time to restore the children's confidence.

Exactly what caused Bruce's reaction we had no idea. Nobody in the hospital had bathed him—he had only been sponged—so we could see no connection between his hospital experience and swimming. But though we could not understand it, we had no alternative but to accept it. Despite all her care, it took Val some eighteen months to restore Bruce's original confidence in the water.

Her second baby, Christine, was born when Bruce was just two years old. She progressed very well, blowing bubbles at four and a half months, and Bruce's tenseness started to ease when he saw his baby sister in the water. For a long time he refused to go near the deep end of the pool, but gradually he overcame this fear, and by his fourth birthday was swimming alone in deep water.

The Frightened Child

In many cases a baby would be happy and confident in the water between the ages of twelve and eighteen months, going happily underwater, submerging his whole face, lying on his back, and doing almost any feat in water. Then winter would come, with its lack of opportunity for swimming, and the following summer that previously confident child would be apprehensive, possibly even actually afraid of water.

The explanation seems to be a matter of normal life experiences. At the age of a year, if his parents' attitude has enabled him to feel confident about himself, he will have an adventurous spirit and will welcome the chance to explore the world of water.

Then, if he is unlucky, a comparatively long period of time follows in which he has no opportunity to be in a large body of water, just at the time when he is beginning to expand his explorations of the world around him. His parents have had to warn him of certain dangers, and inevitably he learns for himself that not everything in the world is safe.

By the time summer comes again, he has acquired a certain wariness of new experiences and to him the water is new. As far as he can remember, last summer might never have happened.

In this situation great care must be exercised. If the child is allowed to reestablish his confidence gradually, all will be well. If, remembering how enthusiastic he was the previous summer, a parent tries to hustle him into the water or refuses to accept the fact that he has good reason to approach the water differently now, he is likely to become more frightened than ever and his reluctance to go into the water will be more deep-seated.

The Child's State of Mind

How do you help a child to achieve a state of mind that will keep him safe in the water? Basically you do it by letting the child know that his feelings and happiness are of prime importance and that swimming itself is only secondary.

Knowing this makes a child feel good. His ego is satisfied and his confidence boosted. Then progress in swimming follows naturally, and usually at an incredibly fast rate.

Take Jane. She was two years old when she started lessons, and her mother conscientiously did all the exercises, urging Jane to copy her. Jane still had not progressed far after some weeks of this, and her disappointed and discouraged mother began to wonder if she ever would. Jane was obviously not tuned in to her mother: most of the time her eyes had a faraway, dreamy look.

I told her mother, "I don't want you to give Jane any instruction from now on. Just cuddle her and play with her. Let Jane lead the way."

The change was little short of miraculous.

Jane took control, directed the play, and told her mother what to do. Within two sessions Jane was doing all the breathing exercises, torpedoes, floats, in short every single thing we had been trying to get her to do through the previous unproductive weeks.

We can only assume that Jane had resented her mother's trying to impose her adult will. Too young to explain her objections in words and too small to resist physically, she reacted by simply tuning out.

Jane became one of our best baby swimmers, loving every moment of her lessons—and her mother loved them, too.

I have seen similar reactions over and over again.

If children can't cope with the environment or the people with whom they must deal, they simply escape to dreamland. The mother is left holding the child's body, but his mind is far away and true communication becomes impossible.

I have seen many parents become so frustrated by this reaction that they resort to physically hurting the child in an attempt to bring him back to reality. Actually, the effect on the child is the opposite. Instead of being shaken back into reality, he simply withdraws further. When a mother screams at a child, repeating the same command several times, he may eventually obey in order to stop the screaming, but so halfheartedly that the result is invariably poor.

It is such a shame. What they don't realize is that teaching their baby to swim can be a wonderful way of establishing a real two-way communication with the child.

I suggest that when you start teaching your baby to swim, you try to do it with other mothers or fathers and their children. Coming together regularly in class creates a bond of friendship between mothers. The babies benefit tremendously from their exchanges of ideas and experiences, and from the relaxed atmosphere as the mothers' friendships develop.

It's interesting to notice what happens to the children when their mothers are talking casually among themselves. Each mother will be keeping an eye on her child, but the intensity of supervision relaxes. The children quickly become aware of this and take advantage of the temporary respite from "learning" to follow their own bents. Older ones start diving underwater, or do beautiful torpedoes across the water; younger ones wearing water wings chase a ball half the length of the pool; smaller babies in the arms of their mothers blow bubbles continuously.

And why not? I am not the first to observe that children tend to react more favorably when they feel that no pressure is being placed on them. When we least expect it the baby all by himself blows beautiful bubbles.

It is impossible to measure progress by individual, consecutive lessons. For a small child, learning to swim is something like doing a jigsaw puzzle. The chld picks up one piece of knowledge one day, another piece another day. Then one day the pieces all fit together, he sees the pictures, and he joins in the exercise the other children are doing.

A child appears to know that he must first learn by watching others, and if he is left to himself he will attempt an action when he considers he has learned enough from watching. Even if he doesn't succeed the first time, he will try and try again—as long as he has initiated the attempt of his own accord.

The interference of an adult will often set a child back at this stage. His enthusiasm dwindles as the adult gives advice that wasn't asked for. Often an adult, with the best intentions in the world, will take over completely, urging the child to attempt something he is not yet ready for. The result is invariably disastrous. The child loses faith in the adult, in that particular exercise, and worst of all, in himself. He not only learns nothing, he also loses self-respect.

One mother came to our classes with two little girls, one of nine months and the other just over three years old. The mother started them together and had difficulty in realizing that the older child had already developed a fear of water while the younger one hadn't. In addition, the younger child had an entirely different temperament and character from her sister's. She was easygoing and amiable, whereas the older child was very sensitive and nervous. Because the mother had little patience with the older child, she tended to come to me during lessons, sensing that I would never push her beyond her capabilities. I would demonstrate actions and tell her she could copy me if she wanted to, but that she didn't *have* to.

I could feel her progressing; her body was losing its tenseness as she started to overcome her very real fear of water. Though she was still holding on to me while we were in the water, she was beginning to want to do things.

Unfortunately, one day while she was tentatively trying a blowing lesson, and being only partially successful at it, her mother said, "Well, if your little sister can do it, so can you," and pushed her head under the water.

With that one action the mother undid all the work I had done with the child during the time we had been together. Even worse, by frightening her she put the child back further than she had been before. I don't think that little girl will ever completely trust her mother in water again. When the mother realized the damage she had done, she said, "Well, it looks as though this is going to take a long time again."

It did indeed—longer than the mother was able to accept in the end. Each time she brought the girls to the pool she was irritated by the older child's apprehension and infuriated when she would scream and go to me for protection if her mother came near her in the water. Though the younger child was progressing well, the lessons were stopped.

Early and Often

Frequency is the key to learning, in swimming as in so many other fields. If you become hot when you are sitting at a beach, it's reasonable to assume that your baby is also hot. So when you go into the water to cool off, take him with you. If you feel the need for another cooling dip an hour later, take him again. A baby gains more from being in the water five times a day for ten minutes at a time than he would from one period lasting fifty minutes.

Climatic differences play a large part in this aspect of swimming. Mothers who live in Hawaii are fortunate, because the ocean is always warm enough for them to take their babies in, even at the age of three months. Northern Europe is difficult; even in the middle of summer the sun is not hot enough to warm outdoor pools or the sea, and indoor pools are seldom heated above 70 degrees Fahrenheit. In the United States, of course, the climate varies greatly from region to region, and most of the heated pools that are available are privately owned.

If it is impossible to take your baby to a heated

pool, invest in a portable pool. A tremendous range of these pools is available, from small plastic rings twelve inches deep to large, sophisticated models in which adults can swim.

Above all, remember that your baby *can* learn to swim, and will love you all the more for teaching him.

PART THREE

The Lessons

Program A		
	2 min.	Blowing bubbles
	5 min.	Floating
		Going under (2-3)
	5 min.	Floating
		Jumps (2-3)
	5 min.	Floating
	———	
	30 min.	Total length of the lesson

Program B		
	4 min.	Blowing bubbles
	4 min.	Going under
	4 min.	Dipping
	4 min.	Torpedoes
	4 min.	Jumping
	10 min.	Floating
	———	
	30 min.	Total length of the lesson

If your baby is between a few weeks and eight months old, try him first on Program A. If you discover that he is reluctant to float on his back, rather than making an issue out of it, simply go on to Program B.

Basically, Program A is for babies who naturally take to floating. Newborn babies always do but many older babies do not. For those who don't, Program B is the appropriate way to begin their lessons.

If your child is more than eight months old, always begin with Program B.

Whatever the age of your baby, you should be aiming to teach him all the exercises in Program B. Every exercise (except for torpedoes) can be tried in your baby's very first lesson, and the program for the lesson remains the same for children up to approximately four years old. But as the child gains in strength, confidence, and coordination, he does more with each exercise.

Never make any lesson longer than thirty minutes. If your baby is obviously happy to stay in longer, then play with him after the thirty-minute period. Babies can, on the whole, cope with learning for only that length of time. Many, in fact, can't last that long. Instead of overtiring your baby, always aim for him to come out of the water wanting more.

GETTING INTO THE WATER

Correct entry into the pool or other body of water is of great importance. Cuddle your baby firmly in your arms as you walk down the steps. Don't hand your baby to a person strange to him already in the pool. Take him in yourself.

With your baby in your arms, lower yourself until your shoulders are underwater. Baby's face should be level with your own or higher. Never let baby's face be lower than your own. You must be able to see the reactions on your baby's face at all times. His reactions are your only infallible guide as to when to stop doing any exercise and cuddle him, or go ahead.

BLOWING BUBBLES

We always blow bubbles first as it is a very gentle exercise, and enables your baby to adjust to the water temperature and to observe his surroundings.

Hold baby upright facing you. Take a *small* breath.

Gently blow a little onto your baby's face.

Keep blowing and lower your mouth into the water. Keep your neck straight while submerging your mouth. Baby can see the bubbles you are making.

Babies learn this exercise purely by copying. You must patiently show this to your baby repeatedly.

This mother holds her baby's hand in front of her mouth so that she can feel the bubbles. Making a noise while blowing bubbles makes the whole thing more interesting for your baby.

My daughter, Andrea, at three and a half months takes a little mouthful of water and spits it out again. This is often done by very young babies trying to copy their mothers blowing bubbles. Mothers should compliment their babies for this, because eventually it will lead to bubbles.

BLOWING BUBBLES *(cont.)*

Older children master this exercise more quickly than young ones.

Here Dominic at two years old blows bubbles beautifully with Mother.

For added security the older toddler may have his feet on the bottom of the pool when doing this exercise.

BLOWING BUBBLES   Checklist

1. Mother must move backward so that baby moves forward head first.

2. Baby must be held upright with baby's mouth close to the water. Mothers often hold baby's shoulders out.

3. Instead of holding their faces toward their babies, mothers often bury their faces downward in the water. The babies then are not able to see the bubbles coming from their mothers' mouths.

4. Babies learn how to blow bubbles only through copying. *Telling* a baby to blow bubbles seldom has the desired effect.

GOING UNDER

Going Under is next in our usual lesson (Program B).

If you blow hard on any young baby's face, he will close his eyes and hold his breath. We make use of this natural reaction. We *always* blow onto baby's face just before he goes under water. This way it becomes a signal. Babies six months and younger quickly learn what the signal means and cope quite happily with going under. Very few young babies ever cry. With happy, relaxed babies we do this in their very first lesson. With babies from six to eight months or older we lower only their mouths in at first, then the nose, then the eyes. We still give them the full signal, i.e. Lift, Lower, and Blow, so that they prepare themselves fully. They cannot cope as easily with going underwater as the younger ones can. So the older the child the slower he or she will learn this exercise.

I lift two-month-old Krista while taking a big breath. Because this is her first lesson, I lift her quite high in the air to make her aware something is going to happen. She can also hear me take a big breath.

I blow hard on her face as I lower her very slowly toward the water.

I *gently* lower her just under the surface, all the time blowing on her face. Your baby should go no deeper than this in the first lesson. I stop blowing while Krista is under-water.

Though Krista was under for only a short moment the experience has startled her a little. This is normal, and shouldn't discourage you from repeating the exercise (in the next lesson).

GOING UNDER *(cont.)*

Here Lara—nine months old—shows what parents can expect from their baby after several months of regular swimming lessons. Lara has become so used to the exercise that her father hardly needs to blow on her face any more.

Her eyes close.

Her father lets her sink until her face is completely submerged.

He then gently lifts her up again.

Eyes still closed, she takes a breath.

And bursts into laughter.

GOING UNDER   Checklist

1. Because mothers are nervous about putting their babies under water they often do either of the following:

    a.   They put the baby under with quick, jerky movements. This is bad because it takes the baby by surprise and he can't prepare himself for going under. This often results in coughing and spluttering when the baby comes up. The whole lift, lower, and blow must be one rhythmic gentle movement.

    b.   Or they hesitate so much that by the time the baby eventually gets underwater he can't hold his breath any longer and gets a mouthful of water.

    The Golden Rule is:

    Make going under one single movement, allowing enough time for the baby to absorb the message that he is about to go under and yet not taking too long so that he can no longer hold his breath.

    If your baby is not coping well with going under, do it only once or twice per lesson until he *gradually* becomes accustomed to it.

2. Many mothers first blow on the baby's face, but then stop blowing *before* he has gone under. You must let your baby go under while you are still blowing.

3. Always blow on your baby's face as you lower him toward the water. *Never* blow on his face when you lift him up out of the water, either before or after submerging.

GOING UNDER: Ups and Downs

When the baby can confidently go under once, we continue on to Ups and Downs. In this exercise, the baby goes under repeatedly. As the baby becomes used to it, he can go under three or four or more times in succession. *Slowly* increase the number until your baby can confidently go under fifteen to twenty times.

The mother sets the pace by the rhythm of her own breathing. Her breathing should be normal, i.e., neither fast nor slow. In the following pages a mother lets her three-and-a-half month old daughter Marie go under twice. Because Marie is so young, she is held by her mother all the time she is under water. As your baby progresses, you may release him for a second underwater. You then pick him up again out of the water to take a breath. This is a gradual process. At first your hands remain on the baby's chest but loosen their grip, then gradually you pull your hands away from his chest.

Very young babies (under six months) will often take a breath only every second or third time they surface. This will not cause any problems, if every time you do the exercise you do it with the same constant rhythm.

You must watch your baby's face very closely. At the very first sign of discomfort stop immediately. You may notice that your baby's eyes are open underwater. This is normal. You must stay in one spot, and the baby must be kept vertical.

GOING UNDER   Ups and Downs

Mother takes a breath and lifts up her baby.

Mother blows out hard onto her baby's face.

While blowing, she lowers Marie toward the water.

She starts lifting her out almost immediately.

As your baby becomes more capable you need to lift him less until eventually just his mouth clears the water for a quick breath before he can be submerged again.

Mother blows.

While blowing, her mother lowers Marie for her second dip and submerges her.

She lifts Marie up again.

And because her mother has decided Marie has had enough, as Marie comes up, mother turns her on her back.

As I have said, when your baby becomes experienced enough you can start to release him under water. Without having to be taught, he will try to kick his way back to the surface. When he becomes capable of getting back to the surface by himself but can't turn his head back to take a breath, you must do it for him. If you repeatedly turn his head back to clear his mouth and nose for a breath, eventually he will do it by himself. Most babies manage to get just their hair out of the water. To reach the point of being able to get their mouths out of the water, babies must practice constantly, to develop the necessary skill, strength, and coordination. Until the age of two and a half or so, babies' heads are very heavy in relation to the rest of their bodies.

Annelies is ten months old. Her mother blows on her face.

She submerges her daughter slowly.

Then releases her underwater.

Annelies starts to kick herself up to the surface.

But she cannot yet clear her mouth.

At this moment her mother picks her up again to allow her to take a breath.

GOING UNDER: Getting a breath

When teaching their children this exercise, parents have discovered that different approaches are necessary. Here are some examples.

Marnie is four months old. Her mother lifts her up while taking a breath.

She blows on Marnie's face, at the same time lowering her into the water.

She submerges Marnie for a moment.

Then as her mother lifts Marnie out of the water, she puts one arm under her back and the other on her chest and tilts her backward.

Marnie is now flat on her back in the water in the floating position.

GOING UNDER: Ups and Downs;
Getting a breath

When Stewart does the ups and downs his father can release him underwater.

He kicks himself up toward the surface.

When the top of his head reaches the surface his father places one hand behind his neck and one under his chin.

His father then tilts Stewart's head back to clear his mouth.

Stewart then automatically goes on his back in the floating position.

GOING UNDER: Ups and Downs;
Getting a breath *(cont.)*

Toby at sixteen months has accomplished the aim of this exercise. He shows here how he can go under after being released by his mother.

He kicks himself up to the surface.

Without help, he then tilts his head back and takes a quick breath.

With complete confidence, he allows himself to sink again.

Then kicks himself up to the surface for another breath.

On the first of January 1974, when Toby was only sixteen months old, he fell into his parents' swimming pool. His mother saw him fall from her kitchen window. She ran to the pool. By the time she got there, by doing precisely what is shown here, he had managed to reach the pool steps and climb out.

GOING UNDER: Ups and Downs; Getting a breath Checklist

1. Don't wait for your baby to take a breath before submerging him again. Mother must set the rhythm.

2. Don't let your own face go under when your baby's goes under. By doing this you become incapable of closely watching your baby's face for signs of discomfort.

3. Don't lift your baby too high out of the water. It will result in his sinking too deep under. We try to simulate as much as possible what would happen if the baby fell into water alone. In those circumstances, after the first swim to the surface and first breath he would not sink much deeper than just his hair under water.

4. Remember: close communication between parent and child is vital at these moments. If you step in too soon your baby's progress is held up. If you leave your baby struggling too long, he may be traumatized. The best bet for parents is when in doubt, help. Your baby's happiness is the most important thing.

DIPPING

This exercise can be done with all babies in the very first lesson. The difference between this exercise and Going Under is that Mother walks backward continually.

If your baby is having his first lesson you should not submerge him any deeper than his nose. (See first photo on next left-hand page.) As your baby becomes more confident, allow his face to sink a little more under water. (see first photo on next right-hand page).

As your baby becomes more confident, he can stay under longer. He will also need less time to rest between dips.

With a scared two-year-old, an abbreviated dip is an excellent introductory exercise. He will love the movement through the water, and his face need not go under at first. As with a baby, you should hold him by the chest until he gains confidence.

In the first series of pictures that follow Marie is three and a half months old.

DIPPING

Marie has done this exercise many times.

Her mother raises her and blows.

Her mother lets her sink into the water.

Marie goes under completely.

And comes up again with no fuss.

DIPPING *(cont.)*

When the baby happily goes completely under for a fair amount of time, you can change the way you hold him. The way shown in these photographs offers less security but allows him more freedom of movement and better balance in the water.

Hold the baby's upper arms as shown here.

Lift and blow.

Lower his face into the water.

While your baby is still under water keep holding his arms but loosen your grip.

This may take your baby a little by surprise as he is really floating face down alone after you have relaxed your grip. Therefore release him very gently to avoid startling him.

Lift him out, and start the exercise all over again.

DIPPING *(cont.)*

When your baby happily copes with staying under water while you relax your grip you may *start* on this next step.

Hold your baby by his shoulders. Lift and blow.

Lower him into the water.

While he is submerged release your grip completely. *Do not* remove your hands more than an inch or so from your baby's arms. You must be able to grip them instantly if your baby shows any signs of unhappiness.

At first your baby may sink a little, but as he becomes more experienced he will kick and thrash with his arms, which will help to keep him nearer the surface.

After a moment, grip his arms and raise his face out of the water for a breath. Then start all over again.

DIPPING   Checklist

1. When first starting this exercise, give your baby a long recovery time. Wait until his breathing is completely relaxed before putting him under water.

2. *Gradually* make the time under water longer and the time allowed to take a breath shorter. Your guide is always your baby's face.

3. Don't forget to walk backward. Even when children have mastered this exercise and are in fact "swimming alone," it is very reassuring for them to have their parents walking in front of them, and it encourages them to stay afloat on their own as long as possible. Usually young babies kick vigorously right away, but it is only babies older than eighteen months that use their arms as well as their legs.

4. Remember to hold your baby horizontal in the water.

TORPEDOES

This exercise is usually tried first in about the third lesson.
The baby must be moderately happy about going under.

Marnie is four months old. These
two photos demonstrate how to hold
your baby for a torpedo.

I hold my left hand on Marnie's
tummy. My right hand is behind her
neck with my arm along her spine.
She is firmly sandwiched between
my two arms.

TORPEDOES *(cont.)*

Sally is also four months old. Holding her just as I held Marnie, I blow and lower her toward the water.

Once her face is submerged, I push Sally toward her mother.

I release Sally and she floats alone toward her mother for a very short moment.

Sally's mother places her hands under Sally.

And *gently* (never jerk baby out suddenly) picks her up for a reassuring cuddle and compliment.

This is a torpedo.

TORPEDOES WITH RECOVERY

When your baby is happy to stay under for a considerable time you can teach him the recovery.

I take a breath.

Blow on baby's face.

Place him in the water and give him a gentle push toward his mother.

The baby floats toward his mother.

This time his mother rolls her baby over onto his back.

The baby takes a breath on his back while being held by his mother. When repeating this exercise make sure you always roll your baby to the same side.

Hamish, nine months old, has done torpedoes many times. Here he shows you what you can expect from your baby. His father holds him with one hand on his neck and the other on his chest.

He tilts Hamish over the water, and Hamish takes a breath. His father does *not* have to blow on his face any more.

His father puts Hamish's face in the water and gives him a gentle push toward his mother.

Hamish is all on his own moving toward his mother from the momentum of his father's push.

Still moving!

As he nears his mother, he begins to lift his head out and roll himself over.

His mother reaches out to help him.

And he is over!

TORPEDOES WITH RECOVERY *(cont.)*

If your baby is unhappy about being *rolled* over onto his back try this:

Mother puts Lara's head in the water.

She pushes her baby toward her father.

Lara floats alone for a moment.

Dad places his hands on her ears.

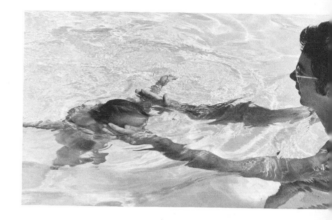

He then lifts her head up and back so that she can take a breath.

TORPEDOES, ADVANCED

You will find that as your baby repeats this exercise he will first float when he is pushed forward, then he will start to kick and eventually he will use his legs, arms, and whole body. The most wonderful part is that you will *not* need to teach him how to use his legs or arms. Baby does this instinctively. If baby is allowed to do this often it will develop into a beautifully well co-ordinated stroke that looks like a dogpaddle.

Generally babies love swimming toward steps. It gives them a feeling of independence. If you are alone in the water with your baby you can also use a toy for him to swim to.

Annelies at fourteen months old cannot yet swim alone in the middle of the pool because she is not yet strong enough to lift her own head up for a breath.

But Annelies can swim a short distance from her mother.

She heads toward the steps.

When she reaches the steps she starts crawling up them.

Her head is out.

And soon all of her is out of the water. She did it all by herself.

TORPEDOES:
A Common Problem

Annelies demonstrates a common inclination among two-year-olds to do a u-turn. She leaves her mother.

She almost immediately starts to turn around.

Her mother redirects her forward.

If you constantly correct your baby's homing instinct, he will eventually learn to swim in a straight line.

TORPEDOES to safety

You should make torpedoing toward the wall part of the torpedo lesson—in case one day your baby accidentally falls into any body of water.

Jennifer is held up for a breath. She can see the wall in front of her, but it is a few yards away.

She swims forward with her mother walking beside her (this lessens the inclination to "home in" on her mother).

Her mother helps her up for a breath.

Then she submerges and swims. All this time she can see the wall getting closer.

She reaches the wall. Her mother helps her put both hands on the wall.

Her mother lets her stay there for a while entirely alone so that she learns to "hang on." All babies over ten months should be taught how to hold onto the wall. It is excellent safety training.

TORPEDOES Checklist

1. It is very important that baby's face be placed down onto the water. Do not push baby's face through the water while he is looking forward. He must learn to swim with his eyes looking down toward the bottom of the pool. This is most important for his body balance.

2. Baby must be pushed forward along the top of the water. Never push baby deep down underwater.

3. Unless your baby is very experienced, always blow on his face just before he goes down.

4. Keep a firm hand on his tummy. If your hand slips up to his chest, you will lose control and squeeze your baby's neck.

JUMPING IN

We do this with *all* our babies right from the very first lesson.

If your baby is very young or apprehensive, sit baby on edge of pool—not too long as baby could get cold. Notice how my fingers hold his head vertical.

Lift baby gently into pool, always keeping his body straight.

Baby should enter the water very slowly. But don't get his face wet yet. Allow baby to get used to the sensation of coming from a height into water. Most babies love this.

Then slowly turn baby onto his back in the water.

And let him have a bit of a float.

Always follow every single jump you ever do with your baby by turning him onto his back. Keep him on his back for quite a while. By doing this repeatedly it becomes a habit for baby to turn onto his back so that in an emergency he will do it automatically.

JUMPING IN *(cont.)*

When your baby has become used to going under you can let him go under with the jump. You *must* give baby the signal that means "You are about to go under"—that is, blow on his face.

Her mother sits Marnie on wall of pool. Because Marnie can keep her head straight her mother uses only her thumb to keep her body vertical.

As she lifts Marnie off the wall she takes a big breath.

Her mother blows onto Marnie's face and then lowers her toward the water.

She keeps blowing while Marnie enters the water.

Because this is Marnie's first time going under with the jump, her mother lets only half of her face go under.

Mother then turns Marnie onto her back.

Mother sits Sally on pool edge.

Sally is lifted in while her mother blows on her face. Notice how she screws up her face.

Unlike Marnie, Sally goes completely under. She has been swimming for three months.

You may gradually let baby go deeper and deeper underwater. At first hold baby firmly. Then slowly loosen your grip while baby is submerged. This motivates baby to start kicking to reach the surface. This again is a gradual process until you can release baby completely.

When Sally's head is out . . .

. . . her mother turns her onto her back.

JUMPING IN *(cont.)*

Stewart is going to jump in all by himself.

Stewart holds his father's fingers, to make sure that when he jumps he will not hit his head on the edge of the pool.

Stewart jumps.

Stewart goes under completely alone.

It is now up to Stewart to kick his way back up to the surface.

When his hair comes out his father extends his arms to help.

Stewart's father then turns him onto his back.

JUMPING IN *(cont.)*

Melissa, one year old, is on the pool edge and is invited in by her mother. This is an important safety rule. Children should be taught to jump into the pool only when invited by an adult to do so.

Like most young babies, Melissa throws herself forward, landing on her tummy.

The easiest way for a baby to get his face out after a belly landing is to roll over.

Melissa's mother places her hands over Melissa's ears underwater.

And starts to roll her over.

Melissa's face is now out of the water.

Her mother then helps her to have a little float.

Jennifer is twenty months old. She is now steady enough on her feet to do the jump from a standing position. Her mother urges her into the pool.

Her mother holds onto one hand to make sure Jennifer clears the edge.

Because she has jumped from a standing position she sinks quite deep.

She takes some time to kick herself
up to the surface.

When her head is clear of the water,
Mother places a hand under Jennifer's chin.

And lifts Jennifer's chin up to clear
her face.

Jennifer then floats for a moment on
her back, holding on to her mother's
hand.

Dominic at two and a half confidently jumps from a standing position into the pool.

He lands on his tummy. For this reason, even older babies like Dominic should not be allowed to jump from heights such as diving boards.

He starts moving his arms and legs immediately, yet we have *never* given him any instructions on what to do with them.

Dominic has no problem clearing his face to take a breath.

His head sinks again, but he keeps moving toward the side of the pool.

Dominic reaches the poolside.

He holds on by two hands.

And pulls himself out.

JUMPING IN Checklist

1. The mother sits the baby on the edge of the pool. Then when the baby jumps in the mother catches the baby in mid-air. This is uncomfortable for the baby. Either hold baby all the way or pick him up gently when he is underwater to help him come up and onto his back.

2. A mother often is so eager to get her baby on his back that she does it before he is even in the water. It is important that the baby be allowed to go in and under first. Only after he has surfaced should he be turned on his back.

3. Until children are two years old it is wise to let them jump only from the sitting position. Particularly when wet, a baby is likely to lose his balance if he is standing up.

4. WE *NEVER*, NEVER, NEVER THROW OUR BABIES IN, NO MATTER WHAT THEIR AGE. WE FEEL IT IS PSYCHOLOGI-CALLY *DISASTROUS.*
   It damages the child's confidence in water and harms the relationship between parent and baby.
   Many older babies who resent being ducked underwater love jumping in and happily let themselves go right under. It is often the only way they will allow their faces to go underwater.

FLOATING

This is the exercise that absolutely amazes people.

They cannot believe their eyes when they see a seven-month-old baby floating entirely alone.

By learning how to float babies become capable of saving their own lives. The youngest baby we ever had capable of saving his life by doing ups and downs by himself was Dominique, at eighteen months old. Yet we have had numerous eight- and nine-month-old babies capable of jumping off the side of the pool, turning onto their backs, and floating alone.

The younger the baby, the more easily he learns how to float. Under eight months is best. Babies older than eight months often resist learning to float because they are too interested in what's going on around them.

Until your baby is strong enough to support his own neck muscles—which is usually three and a half to four months old—you will need to support his neck for him.

To acquire the skill of floating alone requires much practice. The baby must learn through repetition. For this reason we devote at least ten minutes per lesson to floating. If your baby seems to like floating—and each baby is different—spend the major part of the lesson practicing this skill until it is perfected.

Also, every day in the bathtub your baby should practice floating. (See bathtub section, p. 143.) Until your baby is four to five months old the bathtub is big enough. When your baby is approximately eight months old he will be able to touch the sides of the bath when he stretches his arms. That is why he must be given plenty of practice in floating before he reaches that age.

Floating is very difficult for some babies to learn, especially older babies. So if you are starting to teach your baby to swim and he is over eight months old, expect to have much more difficulty. On the other hand, *do* keep trying.

FLOATING ALONE

Holding Marnie close to me at eye level, I spread my hand.

I place it over Marnie's neck. I have good control over her head movements because my thumb and middle finger are just under her ears.

Still holding her close to me I lean over with her toward the water. My left hand is on her bottom.

Now I slowly let her go down into the water away from my body.

She is supported at her neck and bottom. Her ears are in the water, her arms outstretched, the rest of her body nicely relaxed. My right hand supports her neck muscles.

I take away my left hand, and she floats with only my hand on her neck. My body creates a shadow to cover her face. This is most important when teaching in an outdoor pool.

FLOATING ALONE *(cont.)*

Baby must be happy and completely relaxed on his back before you make any attempt to let baby float alone. Baby's body must be stretched so as to distribute his weight evenly along the surface of the water. Baby must be looking straight up to the ceiling, sky, or your face above his own. Baby's ears must be in the water, arms outstretched. Babies who master floating usually stretch their legs straight. This is, however, not so vitally important. Some babies can float with their legs relaxed. The control over floating is governed mainly by the head, chest, and arms. If the baby tries to sit up he will sink. If he arches his spine backward, his face will go under.

These photographs show how to prepare your baby to float alone.

The baby should have arms outstretched, legs fairly straight, tummy up. When the baby is in this position, then, very, very slowly remove your hands a little.

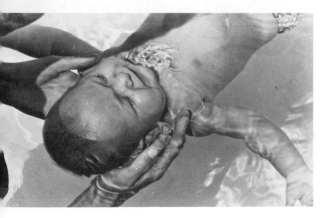

My hands are just to the side and under the baby's head. This way the baby is floating—and yet if she were to drop her head back, my hands would prevent her from going right under.

Marie at three months is typical of babies her age who have had some experience floating. Her mother supports her head slightly with both hands.

Mother removes her hands slowly so that Marie now floats alone.

FLOATING ALONE *(cont.)*

This photo shows exactly what so often happens when the mother removes her hands. The baby's head drops back, and his arms come up. No baby can float with his arms out of the water. The weight of the arms, instead of being carried by the water, is now transferred to the head and body, causing them to sink. Often babies drop their heads back because their neck muscles are not yet strong enough.

The mother just places her hands under the baby's head to lift it up again. If the baby is not upset with having gone under this lifting of the head only is sufficient. If the baby is upset, lift him up and cuddle him. It could be he got some water in his nose which is uncomfortable. So as to prevent the baby from dropping his head under water we prefer his mother never to remove her hands any farther than one inch away from baby's head.

When babies are this young it is the *ideal* time to teach them to float. Right here Marie is neither floating alone nor being held constantly. Learning to swim is very much done through feeling.

As we cannot see ourselves swim we must be directed by what feels right.

With her mother's hand being there to catch her when necessary, the baby is virtually free to explore and learn through what feels right and what results she gets when she moves herself in the water.

Babies can float only when their arms are outstretched to act as stabilizers.

FLOATING ALONE: Common problems

If your baby is very young and yet he won't relax on his back, you may need to burp him. It is impossible for a baby to bring up wind while floating. If that doesn't settle him either, you may need to hold him close to you so he can feel you. Allow him to clutch one of your fingers in his hand.

Babies find it easier to learn to float in an indoor pool where there is no sun shining in their eyes. However, you can teach your baby outdoors if you use your body to provide shade for baby's face.

To make floating a more interesting time, we suspend big blown-up Disney characters from the ceiling above the pool for the babies to look at in our indoor pools. We also sing and talk to our babies.

Constant practice is absolutely essential. Babies who float quite happily at five or six months can become interested in their toes when eight months of age. As it is impossible for a baby to float when his hands are clutching his feet, it is essential that a good floating habit be established before eight months of age. This is the *only* time you are ever firm with your baby. Be gentle, be loving, but be firm.

FLOATING ALONE: Common problems
(cont.)

We have had babies who could float beautifully and for any length of time. Then, when these babies had a break in their regular swimming lessons for whatever reason (illness, vacation, etc.), they completely lost their ability to float. So try to avoid any break in your regular lessons. If a break is unavoidable, practice floating in your bathtub (see chapter on bathtub lessons). If then your baby still has lost his desire to float, you may have to place him on his back and leave him there. Stay close by, of course, and don't allow him to become too upset. But unless you do this your baby may not float again until much, much older. Many of our babies have lost their ability to float because we were not insistent enough at that crucial time.

Babies never cease to amaze me. Many a time I have seen a baby sink, come up to float and take a breath, sink again, and surface again. Quite happily. It often appears that they are trying to teach themselves how to cope with new situations. If I go under while floating, I cannot just right myself as babies can, for my nose becomes uncomfortably blocked with water. This doesn't seem to worry babies nearly so much as adults. But be very observant at this time. First give your baby a chance to work it out for himself. Only if he seems to be becoming upset pick him up for a cuddle. If you cuddle him upright this will also clear his nose.

Many hours have to be spent just letting the baby lie on his back. Here Christian, six months old, demonstrates.

He has to experiment a lot for himself. Often the baby will lift his arm up. This will cause him to sink.

He will learn to stretch his body again so as to float.

FLOATING ALONE *(cont.)*

Because babies are already individuals at birth we must experiment with every baby to find the best way to teach them.

Some babies do not like their heads touched while floating. Jennifer will float only when her mother holds her hips. Many of our babies prefer it this way. Again the mother *slowly* releases her hands when the baby is lying relaxed.

Some babies prefer to look at their mother's face. When the baby is relaxed, slowly remove the arms supporting him, but no more than one inch away from his head.

Some babies continually try to sit up. To remedy this, hold the baby as shown here. He will look back at your face.

Christian mastered floating when four months old. His mother always supported him with only one hand.

When she releases him he stretches his body well and floats. Even when the baby is an accomplished floater do not stay too far from him.

Watch his face all the time. Talk to him and compliment him.

This photo was made for only one purpose: to prove to doubting Thomases that it is possible for a very young baby to float alone. *However*, we seldom move as far away from our babies as Christian's mother has done here because our babies like company. We talk or sing or hold toys above them so as to keep communicating. It must be fun time. We do not want our babies to become lonely.

FLOATING ALONE, ADVANCED

When your baby can float alone reasonably well, you must then teach him how to get his body into the floating position by himself.

In the section on ups and downs you were shown how a baby is taught to surface onto his back when he is underwater in the upright position.

In the chapter on jumping, you were shown how to teach a baby to roll over from his tummy onto his back so as to clear his face and float. When you repeatedly roll your baby over he will eventually learn to do it alone.

Here Christian shows that he has learned.

Christian's mother gives him the lift, blow, and lower signal telling him that he is about to go under.

Christian's mother places him face down on the water and releases him.

His mother removes her hand completely. Christian realizes he is alone.

Christian begins to take action to cope with the situation. He stretches himself.

He raises his right arm and is beginning to roll over.

Christian's right arm is now out of the water.

He has now rolled over completely, but his face is still submerged.

Christian has been able to lift his face out to float. Notice that the body and legs are stretched to distribute his weight evenly along the surface of the water. Many adults cannot do what Christian has just done here. Yet Christian was only six months old when these photos were taken.

FLOATING ALONE: The reluctant floater

If your baby is reluctant to go onto his back, try giving him a bottle in the pool (always use an unbreakable plastic bottle. Glass near a swimming pool is dangerous). Do this at the end of the lesson.

Here I demonstrate with Grant how to do it. Grant rests in my left arm. With my right hand I hold the bottle so that his head is well back and his ears in the water. My body makes shade for his face.

As he isn't going to go under again anyway, it is quite safe to give the baby a bottle of formula, milk, or juice without much risk of upsetting his stomach. Babies use an unbelievable amount of energy while swimming. You will probably find that although it may not yet be time for the baby's feeding he will be ready for it anyway.

Sometimes it's because a baby is hungry or thirsty that he refuses to float. By giving him a bottle you make him feel content. He is more likely to continue floating then, even when he has emptied his bottle.

All your baby s attention is on the bottle. He is not so aware that he is on his back and that his ears are in the water. He is becoming used to the *feeling* of being on his back.

Many of our babies have used so much energy during the lesson and are so content that during floating time they fall asleep. Should this happen to your baby, make sure you allow him to sleep as long as he wishes to. But do *not* release your baby to float alone at this stage, for that would surely wake him and he may never relax to the same degree again.

When Krista can't settle on her back, we give her a pacifier to relax her.

A third method.

FLOATING ALONE: Reluctant older floaters

Here I demonstrate what to do with a toddler or older baby who is reluctant to go onto his back. Start off by holding the baby in a tight cuddle.

Lean over with the baby. Place your hands over his ears.

Then place his head in the water.

Never struggle with your baby. The moment your baby resists, ease up and cuddle. Then repeat the process. Doing the same thing with your baby many times for a short moment is better than forcing your baby to stay on his back. Remember: *Don't rush but don't rest.*

Happiness and togetherness are the results of good baby teaching. Here I am with my very first pupil—our daughter Andrea. Here she is six months old. She floats happily on her back while I stay close to talk and laugh with her.

FLOATING ALONE   Checklist

1. Parents often give up too easily. If baby isn't interested try to make it interesting. Tell a story, sing a song, make funny noises. Do anything, but don't give up. No matter how old your child is, *keep trying.* It may one day save his life.

2. When mothers first start they are often inclined to lift the baby's head too high out of the water. This is uncomfortable for him and gives him incorrect balance. All he needs out of the water is his nose and mouth.

3. With a young baby you need support only his head—not his bottom, body, or legs.

4. When your baby is in the correct floating position, you must spend some time letting him lie there while you still touch him. Then, when you feel he is confident enough on his back, release him *slowly.* Many mothers release the baby so fast that it frightens him. Then you may have quite a job getting him on his back again.

5. Babies whose mothers do *not* bother to practice the floating in the bathtub between lessons seldom learn to float. Floating is a skill acquired only through regular practice.

THE BATHTUB

As most families do not have a heated swimming pool in which they can swim daily, the bathtub is the next best thing both for preparing the baby for swimming in a public pool and practicing in between lessons.

Never use a baby bath. Even when your baby is newly born use the bathtub.

Make sure your baby does all the swimming exercises in clean, clear water. Only when he is ready to come out should you quickly soap and rise him. *Never* allow your baby to swim or play in soapy water.

I like the baby to practice for twenty to thirty minutes daily if possible. This uses a lot of energy. Consequently the baby would become very uncomfortable if you were to bathe him just prior to feeding. Most babies under four months are awake only a few hours a day. Many babies have that time in the late afternoon when they remain awake between feedings. Use this time to bathe your baby. Make sure your baby is well fed and well rested.

The parents of one of our babies moved to a country property when he was nine months old. We didn't see him again until he was twenty months old. Yet in spite of not having been in a swimming pool all that time he was able to do long torpedoes, dip alone, and floated happily. His mother had worked with him in the bath half an hour every day. His confidence and happiness in water were a pleasure to see.

THE BATHTUB

Bathtub exercises are divided into two groups:

    1.   Those you can do with your baby while you remain out of the tub.

    2.   Those you do with both you and baby in the bath.

1. Exercises with you out of the bath.
   A.   Back float.

    Support baby with one hand under his neck and one hand on leg nearest you.

    Gently move him backward and forward along the surface of the water. Be careful not to let any water wash over baby's face.

    Note: The bath is filled as much as possible without overflowing.

    When your baby is quite used to being moved along the top, try the next exercise.
   B.   Waves.

    Hold baby's neck and the leg nearest you.

    Again move baby backward and forward along the surface, thus creating waves. Be careful not to let any waves wash over baby's face as they come toward his face from his feet. The water would flow into his nose and make him very uncomfortable.

    Now allow one wave to flow from the top of his head over his face toward his feet. The water will not enter his nose this way. If your baby shows no sign of discomfort after this exercise, he is ready for going under.

Notice that Byron—four months old—is very calm about going under.

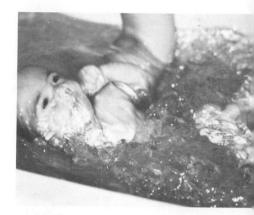

Here Byron's mother is beginning to lift him up. He is actually underwater for only a very short while.

Quite unperturbed, Byron is sitting up. This photo shows how to hold your baby. One sweeping movement is used to let the baby go under and bring him to the sitting-up position.

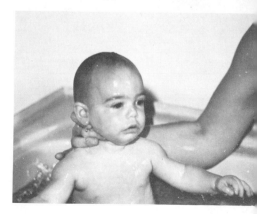

THE BATHTUB *(cont.)*

C. Torpedoes

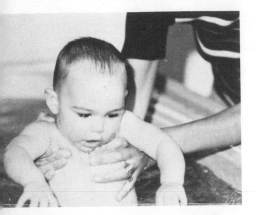

Byron's mother holds one hand on each side of his chest. She blows on his face just before he goes under.

Now she pushes him forward under the water. She does not release her grip.

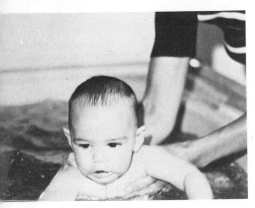

This is Byron's reaction as his mother lifts him up from the torpedo. The position of her hands can be clearly seen.

D. Floating.

Whichever way you usually support your baby in the pool, you can do in the bath. Or you can do it as Byron's mother does here. She first supports him. Then she slowly lets her hand drop a little. This way he floats, but her hand catches him if he should sink. Notice that the bathtub is very full.

Many babies who were very reluctant to float on their backs have gradually become used to it as a result of regular practice in the bathtub. If your baby resists floating in a full tub, try this. Fill it only about six inches deep. Place your baby on his back on the bottom. Make sure that his head is resting on the bottom. There should be enough water to just cover your baby's ears. Now if you give him a bottle with milk or juice your baby should slowly come to accept the back position.

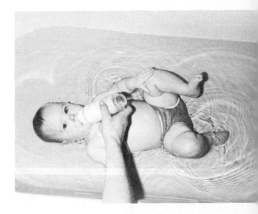

Here Leeanne happily plays on her back. Some of our mothers have hung mobiles on the celling above the bath with good results.

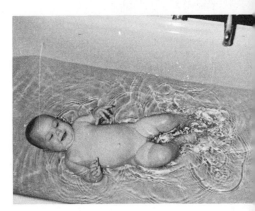

THE BATHTUB *(cont.)*

2. Exercises with Mom or Dad in the bathtub.
    A. Blowing bubbles.

If your baby is very young, this may be the most comfortable way to do it.

If your baby is a little older, it may be more practical to sit him at one end of the tub while you blow bubbles in front of him.

Here Stewart, just twelve months old, does bubbles all alone. *Every* single day he practices this in the bath.

B. Back float, three ways.

Sit up with legs apart. Hold your
baby between your legs facing you.

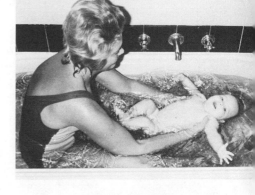

Again the baby floats between your
legs, but now let the back of his head
rest on your tummy. Make sure his
ears are under the water.

Hold your baby in the usual feeding
position in your arms. Either breast-
feed or give him a bottle, but make
sure his position is as near to
floating as possible. This is the most
successful way to get your baby
accustomed to the back position and
having water in his ears.

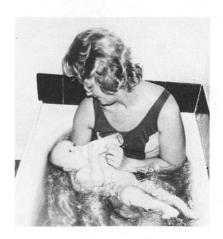

TEACHING AIDS

The greatest teaching aids ever invented were you parents. You, the readers of this book, must realize that parents have long been underestimated as teaching aids just as manufactured articles have long been overestimated.

Our very young babies never use any teaching aids apart from a couple of bathtime toys. Sometimes it is all right to use teaching aids with older babies. These older babies may get the urge to be independent of their mothers before they are really capable of swimming alone. You then may allow your baby to have inflatable armbands on his arms.

Here Jennifer paddles happily with double armbands.

Lara is twelve months old. She is very light and very capable in the water. For her, we have cut the armbands in half so she uses only one compartment of air. As time goes on we will inflate them less and less.

But parents must remember that these inflated armbands generally allow the baby's head to be above the water. Thus the baby never gets the opportunity to discover what it feels like to go underwater or what his own body's relationship to water can be. Especially if parents keep the baby with the bands on all the time, he will develop false confidence in his own swimming ability. If he then jumps in without them on, he is in for a rude awakening.

However, they are excellent for allowing a baby to paddle around by himself after his lesson is finished. They will help to strengthen his kick. Waterwings must be regarded as fun things that a baby can have now and then to amuse himself with.

Never let the baby wear these inflated armbands during the lesson.

TEACHING AIDS *(cont.)*

The only other time we may use the inflated armbands is if we have a baby who won't go on his back and who doesn't like being cuddled. Then we can hold him in any of the three ways being shown below. Because these armbands are rather bulky the baby is inclined to keep his arms outstretched. With the extra buoyancy he will then be able to float when you let go. After doing this repeatedly with armbands on, the baby may then happily stay there as you gradually deflate the armbands and eventually remove them altogether.

Standing in relatively shallow water, I lean over him.

In deeper water, I stand behind him, holding his head. See how close my face is to his.

Again, in shallow water, I hold his head.

Swimming-pool steps can also be a great teaching aid. When our pool in Mount Eliza was built, I insisted that we have steps along the whole width of the pool. Each step was eighteen inches wide. We have three of these steps leading into two and a half feet of water. Many a baby who was apprehensive at first we allowed to play on these steps with a parent. Some babies very quickly ventured onto the second or third step and into the pool. Other babies took a long, long time to build up confidence. From experience I know that every minute spent playing on the steps of our pool was well invested because it helped to build the baby's confidence. Many of the older babies like to swim to the steps and from the steps to their mothers.

Never let a baby play on the steps alone.

TEACHING AIDS *(cont.)*

One of the most effective teaching aids for Annelies is her pacifier.

She swims both on top of the water and underwater.

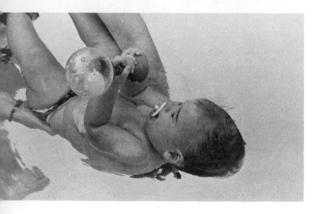

The only way we could ever get Hamish to lie on his back was with his pacifier in his mouth and playing with a toy. After several months he started to relax so much on his back that the pacifier and toy were no longer necessary.

Melissa loves torpedoes toward a big panda.

PLAYING

Playing is important. *Swimming must be fun.*
    This is when the whole family can join in. We encourage parents to play at the end of each lesson.

Here Andrea, Mark, Dominic, and I play ring-around-the-rosy.

Note how Dominic comes up with a big grin on his face.

Joshua watches while I help Phoebe slide down the slide.

Phoebe enters the water feet first.

She goes under and comes up.

Phoebe gets her hair out and turns her head back to breathe. Note the look of sheer enjoyment on her face.

PLAYING *(cont.)*

Annelies likes to play peek-a-boo underwater at playtime.

Dominic's favorite game is swimming through my legs.

Dominic always smiles underwater.

These underwater games are of tremendous value in boosting the child's confidence underwater. Remember, for any child to be truly safe in water it is essential that he enjoy being *under* the water as much as on top.

If there is one thing I want to teach you, the teachers of your babies, it is summed up in this final photograph.

"I'm the BOSS!"